WORLD OF WONDER

Published by Creative Education
123 South Broad Street
Mankato, Minnesota 56001

Creative Education is an imprint of
The Creative Company.

Art direction by Rita Marshall
Design by The Design Lab
Photographs by The Image Finders (Jim Baron, Mark E.
Gibson, Werner Lobert), JLM Visuals (Richard P. Jacobs,
Breck P. Kent), Robert McCaw, James P. Rowan, Tom Stack
& Associates (Sharon Gerig, Thomas Kitchin, Tom & Therisa
Stack), Frank Staub

Library of Congress Cataloging-in-Publication Data

Staub, Frank J.
Photosynthesis / by Frank Staub.
p. cm. — (World of wonder)
Summary: Discusses photosynthesis, the process by which
certain life forms capture the energy of light.
ISBN 1-58341-265-4
1. Photosynthesis—Juvenile literature. [1. Photosynthesis.]
I. Title. II. World of wonder (Mankato, Minn.).

QK882 .S76   2003
572'.46—dc21   2002034839

First Edition

9 8 7 6 5 4 3 2 1

cover & page 1: a rhinoceros eating
page 2: changing leaves
page 3: a spring flower

Creative Education presents

W🌎RLD OF W🌎NDER

PHOTOSYNTHESIS

B Y   F R A N K   S T A U B

Flowers carpet the earth after a fire ❧ Green leaves turn red in the fall 🐈 A houseplant grows toward a window ☀ These events happen because of photosynthesis, the most important process on Earth. During photosynthesis, plants, **algae**, some **bacteria**, and certain other living things use light to make their own food.

ANIMALS DEPEND ON THE food from photosynthesis too since they can't make their own food. Whether it occurs in the mountains, the ocean, or the desert, the photosynthesis process is pretty much the same. But the **adaptations** to carry out photosynthesis take many forms.

Plants flourish in almost all of Earth's habitats

Why are water lilies, ferns, and so many other plants green? The green color is caused by a **pigment** called chlorophyll. Chlorophyll is like a net that captures **energy** from sunlight. Plants use the energy to make food. This is the process of photosynthesis. In Greek, the word *photo* means "light," and *synthesis* means "putting together." Photosynthesis puts together light, water, and a gas called carbon dioxide to form a type of sugar called glucose.

NATURE NOTE: *To move glucose to their various parts, many plants change it into sucrose—a form we know as table sugar. Sugar cane plants contain a lot of sucrose.*

Glucose is the main building block for the substances living things need to grow and function. Plants use some glucose to make cellulose, a substance that makes plants stiff. When a red-winged blackbird lands on a rush, cellulose keeps the plant from collapsing. Plants often make more glucose than they can use right away. So they turn it into **starch**. If a plant doesn't get enough glucose from photosynthesis, it breaks down the stored starch to obtain more.

✳ In addition to glucose, photosynthesis also makes oxygen, the gas that people and animals need to breathe. The air surrounding Earth contained no oxygen until tiny, simple life-forms started performing photosynthesis about three billion years ago. Every bit of the oxygen in the air today was created through photosynthesis.

NATURE NOTE: *Crayfish eat plants, fish eat crayfish, and herons eat fish. This is a food chain. Most food chains depend on food first made by photosynthesis.*

Cellulose gives a bulrush stiffness and strength

UNLOCKING ENERGY

Besides being the starting point for many substances in plants, glucose is the main energy food for every living thing. To unlock the energy in glucose, organisms use a process called respiration. Respiration is like photosynthesis in reverse. It combines glucose and oxygen, the two main products of photosynthesis, and it creates carbon dioxide, one of the main ingredients needed for photosynthesis to occur.

A nutria (a kind of large, water-loving rodent) swimming

through duckweed breathes in oxygen to be used for respiration in its **cells**. As respiration gives the nutria energy, it produces carbon dioxide. The duckweed may absorb some of this carbon dioxide for photosynthesis, which creates oxygen. The duckweed uses some of the oxygen for respiration in its own cells, and the nutria breathes in some of it. In this way, the processes of photosynthesis and respiration form a kind of cycle that helps both plants and animals.

NATURE NOTE: *Animals obtain glucose from their food. Respiration in their cells makes the energy in glucose available for such activities as swimming, fighting, or flying.*

Nutrias and duckweed boost each other's energy

SUGAR FACTORIES

In many plants, chlorophyll is concentrated in the leaves. Pickerelweed leaves, like those of most plants, are flat. This exposes as much chlorophyll as possible to sunlight. Tiny holes called stomata in the surface of each leaf open during the day to take in carbon dioxide and release oxygen.

Chlorophyll breaks down eventually. So plants must constantly make new chlorophyll. But chlorophyll isn't a leaf's only colorful chemical. The

Aspen leaves lose their green color in the fall

leaves of aspen trees and many other plants contain yellow pigments that help chlorophyll absorb light. Although the leaves always contain these bright pigments, chlorophyll usually covers them up. But

NATURE NOTE: *Each leaf on an oak tree contains tens of thousands of cells. Most of these cells contain a lot of chlorophyll for capturing light.*

when fall comes, shorter days and colder nights shut down the chlorophyll-making machinery of plants and trees. Then, with no new chlorophyll to mask them, leaves' yellow pigments show through.

🦎 If fall days are sunny and warm, maple tree leaves continue to work hard making sugar. But if the nights are cold, chemical changes in the leaves cause the sugar to form a red pigment that gives some maples and other plants their flaming fall colors.

SEEKING LIGHT

Plants often compete for sunlight to make food. Picture a thick forest of spruce and fir trees. The dark forest floor has few plants, since it doesn't get enough light for most **species** to

NATURE NOTE: *Slugs chew up leaves that fall to the forest floor. When they get rid of their body waste, they make chemicals in the leaves available for plants to use again.*

make food by photosynthesis. One day a forest fire kills the trees. Sunlight streams down between the burned trunks. Soon, fireweeds decorate the charred earth. Other plants also take root, including pine trees.

❦ Years go by and the pines grow up, eventually forming their own dark forest. As the pines block more and more sunlight, few species can survive under them. But little spruces and firs pop up here and there. Unlike pines and fire-

Wildflowers carpet the forest floor after a fire

weeds, spruces and firs can perform photosynthesis in the
shade. A century later, the
spruces and firs have grown
above the pines and blocked the
life-giving sun. One by one, the
pines starve to death.

  The needle-shaped leaves
of spruces, firs, pines, and other
evergreen trees stay on the
branches all year long. This
keeps the forest floor in con-

NATURE NOTE: *As schefflera
and other houseplants grow,
they curve toward the nearest
window so that their leaves will
face the sunlight.*

A thick spruce forest is too dark for many trees

stant shade, limiting photosynthesis and plant growth. Deciduous trees, by contrast, don't have leaves during cold months. In early spring, before oaks, maples, and other deciduous trees grow their sun-blocking summer leaves, the forest floor is bathed in sunlight. This sparks the growth of grasses and **herbs** such as bloodroot.

When Douglas fir trees

NATURE NOTE: *To produce flowers, a plant needs a lot of food for energy and materials. Painted trilliums make enough food to flower only in early spring, before tree leaves block the sun.*

Spring sunlight brings this bloodroot to life

NATURE NOTE: *Many mountain plants, such as rose crowns and fringed gentians, can perform photosynthesis in colder weather than lowland species.*

crowd together in a forest, so little light twinkles through the treetops that the trees have no lower branches. If leaves can't get enough light for photosynthesis, a tree doesn't need them or the branches that hold them.

☀ A tree such as a Douglas fir growing in the open has a different shape than the same kind of tree in a forest. Trees in the open grow lower branches that

Fir trees' tall trunks are often bare of branches

are often quite long. These branches stretch out beyond the shade of the upper limbs to receive life-giving sunshine. The more leaves a tree exposes to the light, the more food it can make.

NATURE NOTE: *Alpine sunflowers and other high mountain plants are short. Short stems require less food from photosynthesis and help plants avoid the wind.*

Trees may grow in curves to reach life-giving light

SHORT SUMMERS

In the mountains and the far North, summers are short. Winters are long and cold. Photosynthesis shuts down if temperatures drop too low. That's why most of the trees in cold regions are evergreen

NATURE NOTE: *The paloverde, a desert tree, can't produce enough food in its tiny leaves. So chlorophyll in its bark performs about 40 percent of its photosynthesis.*

Deciduous trees store food to survive the winter

conifers such as pines, spruces, and firs. These trees don't have to bother growing new leaves each spring as deciduous species do. As soon as the weather warms up, conifer needles start making food.

🌿 Almost all of the plants found high in the mountains are **perennials**, such as the little sky pilot. Each summer, the sky pilot grows a bit bigger until it's ready to flower. Annuals are plants that live and

NATURE NOTE: *Jojoba leaves stand straight up to avoid facing the midday desert sun. They perform photosynthesis in the mornings and evenings when the low sun strikes their surfaces.*

die in a single season. Annuals are rare high in the mountains. High country summers are just too short for these plants to make all the food they need to grow up from a seed and make flowers before winter returns.

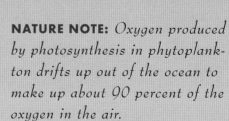

NATURE NOTE: *Oxygen produced by photosynthesis in phytoplankton drifts up out of the ocean to make up about 90 percent of the oxygen in the air.*

HOLDING WATER

A plant can't make chlorophyll and perform photosynthesis without enough water. But land plants are constantly losing water to the air—a process called evaporation. Most of this evaporation comes from leaves, especially big leaves. Desert plants such as the ocotillo save water by having small leaves. Plus, the ocotillo's leaves appear only after a good rain. As the

The ocotillo is well-suited for desert conditions

desert becomes drier, the leaves fall away.

Cactuses have no water-wasting leaves at all—just pointy spines. A cactus makes all of its food in its chlorophyll-rich skin. Stomata in the skin expose the cactus' juicy insides to the thirsty desert air. That's why many cactuses and other desert plants open their stomata to take in carbon dioxide only at night when the air isn't so dry, instead of during the day as most plants do. Of course,

Chlorophyll makes a saguaro cactus' skin green

All of the world's photosynthetic cells together produce about 100 billion tons (91 billion t) of sugar a year.

photosynthesis cannot happen without light. So cactuses change the carbon dioxide slightly to store it. After sunrise, photosynthesis begins using the carbon dioxide that was stored during the night.

Cactuses "breathe" at night when the air is cool

IN THE WATER

Algae are responsible for nearly all of the photosynthesis that occurs in oceans, rivers, and lakes. Large algae in the ocean are known as seaweeds. But most algae are one-celled organisms called phytoplankton. Phytoplankton drift about in the currents. In Greek, *phyto* means "plant," and *plankton* means "wandering." Some scientists think "photoplankton" would be a better name since these wandering algae live only in sunlit waters near the surface. In deeper, darker waters, phytoplankton can't make food.

Photosynthesis occurs in all bodies of water

❋ Although sunlight generally appears to be white, it is actually a combination of colors: red, orange, yellow, green, blue, indigo, and violet. The colors we see are the colors that objects reflect. Objects absorb the colors we don't see. In algae known as green algae, chlorophyll reflects green light and absorbs red and orange light for photosynthesis. Other algae called red algae contain a red-reflecting pigment that absorbs blue light.

❧ When sunlight shines into clear water, red and orange light reach only a short distance below the surface. That's why green algae are limited to wet surfaces and shallow water, where they can receive the red and orange light they need. Blue light, however, may reach down into the water 100 feet (30 m) or more. Because they use the blue light to make food, only red algae can live at such depths.

NATURE NOTE: *Seaweeds known as brown algae grow gas-filled bags. This makes the weeds float upright in the water to expose them to light.*

Seaweed flourishes in clear, tropical waters

FOOD FOR ALL

In the smallest algae and most enormous trees, photosynthesis captures light to make food for energy and growth. This makes food not only for plants, but also for the people and animals that eat the plants. Without photosynthesis, we would have nothing to eat and no oxygen to breathe.

✳ The ability to create food is just one of the countless adaptations that help living things thrive in the challenging world around them. These adaptations are valuable reminders of how intricately the lives of various creatures are intertwined. As humans make changes that affect the environment, it's important to remember and respect these connections. In doing so, we can help ensure the future health and beauty of this amazing world, this world of wonder.

NATURE NOTE: *Pollution adds carbon dioxide to Earth's atmosphere. Plants help to limit the effects of pollution by using some of the extra carbon dioxide in photosynthesis.*

All animals depend on photosynthesis for life

WORDS TO KNOW

Adaptations *are characteristics or behaviors that help a living thing stay alive or have young.*

Algae *are living things that have chlorophyll for photosynthesis, but no roots, stems, or leaves.*

Bacteria *are very small life-forms that break down waste and dead matter; some of them cause disease.*

Cells *are the tiny building blocks that make up all living things.*

Evergreen trees and shrubs that produce cones instead of flowers are called **conifers***.*

Energy *is the ability to do work; all living things need energy to survive.*

Herbs *are plants that contain no wood and die back into the ground each year.*

Perennials *are plants that live more than one year.*

A **pigment** *is a substance that gives color to plants, animals, and other living things.*

A **species** *is a group of living things that can successfully breed with each other.*

Starch *is a white substance that plants make to store energy; the inside of a potato is starch.*

INDEX